Greek M.

The myth of Hercules

Charlie Keith

Published in the United States

Contents

Prologue

A long time ago in a land called Greece, at the top of the legendary Mount Olympus there lived twelve gods, strong and proud, and full with emotions such as any human has. The almighty Zeus was their king, ruler of thunder and lightning, and Hera, his wife, was their powerful queen.

Ruling both mortals and inferior gods the Olympians had many adventures but none knew the world more than Zeus himself. The king of the gods loved the humans, caring and assisting them in any way he could. It's true that he had many children from mortal women, but his most loved one was the son he had with the beautiful lady Alkmene.

He was so happy the day of his birth and nothing could ruin that happiness.

"Nothing?" whispered Hera behind his back.

That goddess was always jealous and hated every child that Zeus had with other women.

"I'll teach him a lesson" she said and without anyone know she sent two snakes in the infant's cradle. But, the son of the king of the gods was special. He grabbed the snakes and choked them with his baby hands playing afterwards with them as if they were dolls.

Alkmene saw that and was terrified. She decided to give the baby a different name. Instead of Alcides, which was her first option, she chose Hera-cles (meaning glory to Hera) in order to appease the goddess. But, the queen of mount Olympus had a heart of ice and didn't like that at all. She thought they were trying to fool her, and became so angry that she made her life's goal to destroy Hercules for good.

Hera's jealousy and meanness was a constant threat for our hero. Zeus was busy – a god?!? knows where – and the rest of the Olympians had business of their own. And with everyone preoccupied, the divine queen forced Hercules to commit a terrible murder, so terrible to describe, that made him sad and miserable. That was her moment of evil joy. But, Zeus soon learned of this and visited his boy to tell him how he could fix the problem he had created.

"You are strong, Herc but slow in taking action" Zeus said to him.

"What do you mean?" he replied.

"I mean that you should do something to atone for your crime"

"Like what?" Hercules glanced at him

"How should I know? If I knew everything beforehand I would never have married that crazy woman in the first place" spoke the king of the gods.

"And what now?" asked Hercules.

"Go to Pythia. She might have an idea or two"

And so, the demigod hero traveled to Delphi to learn how he could redeem himself. Pythia, the oracle of Delphi after she had eaten a lot of laurel leaves had a vision. She advised Hercules to serve the king of

Tiryns, Eurystheus for ten years performing whatever tasks he might set upon him. If he was successful, that is if he was still alive in the end he would be atoned and rewarded with the divine gift of immortality.

But, Hercules, as a strong and arrogant young man didn't like the idea of serving a man so weak and unworthy of respect. He was ready to decline when a thunder struck in the distance and he knew that his father wouldn't allow him to back out. Fearing for his wrath he reluctantly took the assignment.

When he arrived in Tiryns, he spoke with king Eurystheus about his mission. The king however was a true servant of Hera and following orders of his precious goddess thought a labour that was sure to bring Hercules' demise.

"You shall slay the Nemean Lion" he told Hercules.
"Where's that?" Hercules said.
"Not in Nemea" mocked him the king.

"Very funny" growled the hero and left thinking how to find that creature.

1st Chapter: The Nemean Lion

It wasn't hard to discover the cave of the beast. Hercules heard it as it snored inside.

"The lion has eaten" he said to himself "Men or sheep I wonder?"

He took out his bow and provoked it to appear by yelling:

"Here, kitty, kitty. Come out, kitty"

The lion gave a mighty roar that made some of the shepherds nearby to wet their pants and came out to devour the man who interrupted its sleep.

When Hercules saw the magnificent, large lion with the long brown mane (hair) and the bright golden fur he stood for a while to admire it. But as soon as it made to jump on him he didn't hesitate and fired so many arrows that could have made a man look like that well known cheese with the holes. The missiles though bounced off the lion's impenetrable golden fur and fell down. The demigod thought he had missed, and the beast gazing on his surprised face made a fool of him as it turned its back and waved its tail.

"Hey! Stop that!" Hercules was furious.

He quickly followed the beast inside its cave and then a terrible fight started there. In such a closed space the lion was a tough adversary even for the muscular hero, and during the conflict it decided to have finger food, that is one of Hercules' fingers. The son of Zeus seemed to face defeat – so early in his quest - until he grasped his olive wood club and with it smacked the lion in the head, and managed to stun it. He then found the chance to strangle the beast using his supernatural strength thus achieving in his first labour.

After a while, he thought of skinning the lion. He wanted to prove that he had completed the task. He took out his knife but the fur proved too hard for the blade.

"I have forgotten that your flesh is like a rock" he murmured.

And then, out of a sudden, the goddess of wisdom, Athena appeared inside the cave.

"Use one of the lion's claws to take its hide," she said, and as she had come in the same way she vanished from the place.

"Good advice, sister" he thanked and goddess and proceeded with the skinning. It didn't take him long to get the golden hide, and proudly enough he wore it on his shoulders and returned to Tiryns.

When he entered the palace king Eurystheus was terrified at the sight and quickly hid inside a large storage jar (pithos), admitting with dread that Hercules had been successful in his first task.

"Don't be too overconfident" he said from his hiding place echoing like he was in a well.
"The tasks ahead will surely get harder for you."
"If that's the case" Hercules answered laughing
"Get used to the idea of being inside that jar every time you see me"

He prepared for his second labour. but not before he had eaten a nice, large meal that filled his belly and gave him strength.

2nd Chapter: The Lernaean Hydra

A herald of the king Eurystheus approached Hercules.

"Still in the jar eh?" he said with a smile.

"Excuse me?" the herald looked at him baffled.

"Nothing, You wanted to tell me something?"

"Yes. King Eurystheus demands that for your second labour you must slay the Lernaean Hydra"

"Is that so?" Hercules crossed his large arms in front of his broad chest.

"Alright, I will do it" and left the palace.

On his way to lake Lerna, the hero ran into his nephew Iolaus who was fishing in a river.

"Where to, uncle?" the boy came to him.
"I'm off to kill a beast. Do you want to come?" Hercules said, and Iolaus nodded yes.

The two companions followed the river upstream until they reached the dangerous swamps surrounding Lake Lerna. Poisonous fumes filled the air and the stench of death and other foul things (probably from the beast itself) lay heavy all around them.

"Be careful" warned Hercules "The beast's lair is near"
"We should cover our mouths and noses" suggested Iolaus due to the poisonous gases, and they both used clothes for that.

They approached with caution, and came up to a rocky cave between the lake and the swamps. Hercules took out his bow and arrows. He lit a fire and flamed his missiles, firing upon the rocky concentration. The serpentine nine-headed monster slowly but steadily appeared at the mouth of the cave. What a sight!

Hercules didn't wait and rushed forward wielding his sword. He cut off one of its heads and cried out "Triumph!".

But Iolaus interrupted him pointing out: "Eh, I think that thing grows heads"

"What?" Hercules exclaimed and he saw, not without dread, that from the bleeding neck two more heads had sprung up. "This can't be" he stammered and slashed off two more heads only to face now a twelve-headed Hydra. It was beyond than obvious that Hercules couldn't win simply by chopping his way out of this snake mess.

"This is a nightmare!" yelled Iolaus who knee-deep in the swamp could feel his end drawing near. Suddenly, the boy had an idea. Now, whether it was Zeus or Athena or even his wild imagination no one could tell, but his plan was a good one.

"Uncle" he shouted.

"What?" said Hercules exasperated beating the monster with his club, yet to no avail.

"I can't take you back to your mother now. Wait until I'm done here!"

"No, it's not that. I know how to kill it"

"Well, tell me before we're both dead meat here" cried the hero.

"Use fire to cauterize the necks after each cutting," said Iolaus.

"I hope this works!" gasped Hercules and seized his sword.

"Here we go again" he breathed and started cutting heads one more time.

In the meantime, Iolaus who had lit a torch came close after each beheading and with its flame scorched the stumps.

"Wooow! It works," shout Iolaus.
"This is taking forever" Hercules groaned but in the end the beast was dead and he victorious.

"I thought I'd never kill that blasted thing," he said all sweaty and dirty, but thank Zeus the swamps were smellier. He used fire to burn the rest of the monster, but before that he dipped some of his arrows in its poisonous blood.

"Why are you doing that?" asked Iolaus.
"They might come in handy afterward" answered Hercules

"It's getting late. Let's go back. Your mother is going to get sick worry and I do not wish to deal with her"

"She's strong" laughed Iolaus.

"She's invincible" smiled Hercules.

3rd Chapter: The Ceryneian Hind

Hera was infuriated when she learned that Hercules had slain the Lernaean Hydra. Keep in mind that Hydra was one of her favorite pets, after all the goddess herself had raised it specifically to kill the son of Zeus. Nevertheless, she was calmed when she considered two important facts. Firstly, the second labour was declared invalid – King Eurystheus as a true follower of the queen of the gods notified the demigod hero of that, yet not without the terrifying idea of entering the jar again fearing Hercules'

reaction. Secondly, the next labour that Hera had conceived would certainly kill the demigod hero.

"For your next task" said Eurystheus
"I want you to capture and bring to me the Ceryneian Hind. A creature so beautifully divine and majestic that can outrun an arrow"
"It can't be that fast" objected Hercules.
"Well, if you think you can catch it then prove it"
"Fine. I shall bring you the hind, king Eurystheus" the hero said and went to gather provisions for the hunt.

At first light, he departed and traveled to the woods where it was rumored that the Ceryneian Hind was last seen. He searched for the animal there for nearly a year, and just when he was about to think that he would never find it, suddenly, there it was.

"There you are!" he exclaimed
"Let's see if what they say about you is true" and at that ran towards it. Yes, he chased it. He should have

known better because the hind as soon as it saw him coming turned about with a faster than a blink of an eye leap and sprinted swiftly like the wind. In fact, it was faster than that.

"Damn! That's fast!" puffed Hercules watching it vanishing among the trees.
"How am I supposed to capture an animal like that?" he scratched his head and resumed running.

Nearly a month passed that way, with man and animal playing hide and seek, and catch me if you can until the hero devised a plan to capture the hind with his fishing net. He set the net in a thicket of trees and lured the animal there with berries and sweetgrass that smelt like honey. The Ceryneian Hind, no matter how fast it was, couldn't resist a fine meal, and when it came to eating the delicacies it was too late before it realized that all this was a trap set by the son of Zeus. Hercules rushed in from behind a large bush and grabbed it. Finally! He had taken hold of it.

"Yes!" he cried triumphantly.

"I got you now!" But, no sooner had he hoisted the animal on his back when the goddess of the hunt, Artemis showed herself in front of him. She was holding a magnificent bow and a golden arrow drawn back, aiming his head.

"What are you doing with my sacred animal?" she demanded to know.

"Oh, boy" Hercules sighed and started to explain, all the best he could do, that he didn't want to hurt the animal, that its capture was a labour of his to redeem himself, and so on. Artemis didn't believe him at first and she was that close to fire her arrow through Hercules's thick skull. But, the demigod had been lucky because, at that critical moment, the almighty Zeus and his daughter Athena stepped in to vouch for the hero.

"He's a good lad," said the king of the gods.

"You can trust him" added the goddess of wisdom.

"He's half-human. How can I trust him? All humans hunt my animals to skin them and eat them. Hasn't he done the same to the Nemean Lion?" Artemis had her doubts and frankly, no one could blame her.

"I guarantee for him. No harm will come to your hind" Zeus supported his son, and eventually, Artemis was convinced hence permitting Hercules to take the hind with him for a while.

"I want the hind to be free in a month otherwise I'm going to kill you" she warned him and Hercules kept his promise.

Within a week he brought the hind to king Eurystheus and waited for him to say that his labour had been completed.

"Yes, you have succeeded again" he groaned with dissatisfaction and demanded the animal to be carried into one of his cages.

"This hind shall make a great addition to the zoo I'm building" he grinned.

Hercules said that Eurystheus himself should come to take the animal from him. The king started walking towards Hercules and the hind, but Hercules purposefully left the hind loose a moment too early.

"OOPS!"

Hercules let the hind off his hands just before Eurystheus could grab it and with a graceful sprint, the animal had dashed off Tiryns heading back to its sacred grove. The fact that Eurystheus was so close to the Hind when it ran away allowed Hercules to avoid blame for its escape.

In that way, Hercules had completed the labour and also kept his promise to goddess Artemis of not harming the animal and letting it go free.

Angry, Eurystheus told Hercules that the next task he should perform would be to catch the Erymanthian Boar.

4th Chapter: The Erymanthian Boar

The fourth labour of Hercules was the capture of another animal, the dangerous Erymanthian Boar.

"The Boar that doesn't bore and makes centaurs bore?" joked Hercules.

"There's no time for funny comments. Fetch me that wild pig!" demanded king Eurystheus.

"The Erymanthian Boar you mean" teased him the demigod.

"Yes, the boar. Go and get it already!"

"I'm on it" nodded Hercules and left.

He travelled up to the mount Erymanthos where the animal supposedly lived. Near the foothills he met a friend of his, the wise centaur (half human - half horse) named Chiron. Chiron was the trainer of many heroes such as Achilles and Jason, and knew a lot about medicine.

"Hello, Hercules. How have you been? I've heard you are performing tasks for that old fox Eurystheus. But, come to my cousin's adobe and drink some wine with us. I want to know all about your adventures" he welcomed him and walked or rather trotted with him to a cave close by.

"Greetings to you as well, Chiron and to your cousin" said Hercules when he had settled near the fire inside the cave.

"The weather has gone bad during the last few days" he noticed.

"You mean it's cold" joked Chiron's cousin.

"Yes, the winter has come hard on these lands. It will pass as do all the seasons. But what is your business here, my good friend?" Chiron asked him.

"I'm looking for the Erymanthian Boar"

"Eurystheus requested that beast? I thought he was afraid of anything that has claws of talons" noted the wise centaur.

"He still is" laughed Hercules and the centaurs joined in the good mood.

"Well, if you're looking for that boar you're in the right place alright. But I doubt you'll catch it easily. It's fast" told him Chiron.

"I have chased faster creatures before" said Hercules as he remembered the labour of the Ceryneian Hind.

"Anyway, if I were you and wanted to catch the Erymanthian boar I'd corner it in deep snow where he wouldn't be able to move" Chiron gave him a hint and Hercules thanked him.

"Let's drink some wine now" the other centaur suggested and brought a bottle. But, when he opened it, the smell was so strong that it drew to it other centaurs who happened to cross outside the cave.

"That stuff makes you drunk just by smelling at it" cried one as he entered galloping inside.

"Give it to us! Give it to us!" said others running like crazy horses.

"Easy, brothers!" shouted Chiron who took the bottle from his cousin's hands and exited the cave.

"You want that?" he showed them the wine.

"Go and take it!" and threw it far in the forest under the mountain. The maniac centaurs ran towards it and they were never heard of.

"Well, that is settled. We should probably rest now. I'll stand guard" Chiron said upon his re-entry.

Hercules rested well that night in the centaur's cave without any more trouble, and in the morning he said farewell to his friend and climbed the mountain to seek the Erymanthian Boar.

By noon he had found it roaming near a spring and quickly pounced on it. The beast got away and Hercules hunted it down driving it towards the higher areas where the snow had already set in. Nowhere to run to the boar dived inside the snow and soon enough it got stuck.

"Piece of cake" smiled the hero and seized the boar, tying its feet together. He lifted it up on his shoulders and began the trip back to Tiryns.

"Don't worry, my little friend. No one's going to make bacon out of you" he reassured the frightened animal.

When after a week or so Hercules arrived at the palace and showed the captured boar, king Eurystheus got so afraid (more than the boar itself) that he immediately ran and hid again inside his storage jar.

"Take that monster away! Take it away!" he yelled to Hercules.

"Does he always get that scared of animals?" Hercules asked one of the king's advisors.

"Yes" the advisor answered with a chilled voice.

"I thought he wanted to open a zoo. What kind of a zoo manager is scared of animals?" said Hercules, but to that he got no reply. He went outside Tiryns and released the boar.

"Go now, my little friend and eat nuts and roots and whatever else it is you're eating. Go, you are free' he said having thus completed the fourth labour.

5th Chapter: The stables of king Augeas

The next objective for Hercules was to clean the stables of King Augeas. Now this feat seemed impossible even for a hero with divine blood running in his veins. Nonetheless, Hercules visited the stables in order to evaluate the situation. Too bad for him.

King Augeas owned more cattle than anyone in Greece. Some say that he was a son of one of the great gods, and others that he was a son of a mortal; whosever son he was, Augeas was very rich, and he had many herds of cows, bulls, goats, sheep, and horses.

"By the gods of Olympus," he shouted feeling like he was about to throw up. He exited the place, away from all this immense dung, and went down to a river nearby to wash his hands. When he was able to breathe again he complained about the filth of that place.

"What a stench! The Hydra's swamps were far cleaner than these stables. Dear Zeus!"

"What is it?" said his father who appeared out of nowhere "What is that stink?"

"Nothing. I have this under control" uttered Hercules and Zeus holding his nose disappeared.

"Disgusting" muttered the hero as he started to think of ways to clean that horrid mess. That took him a while until upon gazing at the running water close to his feet came up with a brilliant idea.

He went back, held his breath, and flung open the two large doors of the stables. After that he left running up the hill, the odour helped him in that and stopped near the river.

"The water will wash out all this dung!" he said and quickly enough he gathered heavy boulders from a stone mine close by, and plunged them into the river thus rerouting its course and making it rush straight through the stables down in the valley.

"It's bath time!" he shouted watching as the torrent, which sounded like a thunderstorm swept everything in its path.

The establishment was thoroughly cleaned together with the animals that infested it, and the king Augeas himself. All, everything was clean when the waters subsided.

"What a tsunami was that?" exclaimed king Augeas with water dripping from his beard. His white robe was whiter than the summer clouds.

"Who can say no to a nice bath?" remarked Hercules checking to see if the stables had been entirely cleansed.

"Perfect" he said.

"You have done me a great service, Hercules" told him king Augeas "Take this pouch of gold"

"Thank you" Hercules accepted the gold. "All this exercise with the rocks upstream made my stomach growling for food"

"Oh, if you go to the tavern further down the valley you'll find some excellent dishes to satisfy your hunger" proposed king Augeas.

"Really? What kind of dishes?" Hercules asked.

"Oh, just this morning I sent over some of my sheep. You'll find their meat delicious"

"Ah, I think I'll eat some vegetables instead" said the demigod, who could still smell that disgusting odour of the stables.

Hercules ate five dishes of eggplants, cucumbers, tomatoes and other veggies before he left for Tiryns to announce the completion of his fifth labour.

6th Chapter: The Stymphalian Birds

"Stymphalia" said King Eurystheus.

"What about it?" frowned Hercules sensing what might come next in his labours.

"I want you to eliminate the birds that lurk there" ordered the king.

"You want me to bring them all here?" joked the hero trying to lift his spirits.

"No! no!" shuddered Eurystheus.

"Just kill them, drove them away, do whatever you see necessary until they no longer pose a threat to the area"

"Very well" nodded Hercules and off he went.

He reached the lake Stymphalia and there saw the dangerous birds that terrorized the surrounding area for years flying above his head. He noticed that they were black in color, had razor edge feathers and bronze beaks.

"Formidable" he muttered and proceeded, but it wasn't easy to find their nests. He searched and searched but with no success.

"Where are those nests?" he sighed and the goddess Athena came again to his aid.

"The god of war Ares created these vile birds, and now he can't seem to remember how to control them. I've come to give you a hand. Here" she said and handed him a rattle.

"You know what to do" she added and left him.

"Of course I do" he muttered and put the rattle inside his cloak.

Hercules walked closer to the lake and entered the marshes. Mud and reeds slowed him down.

"I believe now is the time," he said and shook the rattle. A piercing sound echoed all around. So much that Hercules covered his ears. And then, a cloud of these terrible flying creatures rose in the air. Startled by the incredible noise they soared screeching in panic. From that point on everything was easy. Hercules shot down a great deal of them with his bow before the rest of the flock or what remained of it fly away and desert the place. They were never to return again.

"Mission accomplished" noted the hero and went back to Tiryns.

"So?" said the king when he saw him.

"Have you eliminated the threat?"

"Yes" answered Hercules.

"How?" Eurystheus wanted to know.

"I found a rattle" the demigod started to say and in doing so he took out the rattle from under his lion's cloth.

"And I shook it like this" and moved it in his hand filling the palace of Tiryns with the same terrifying sound that had scared the birds. Everyone fell down and tried to close their ears.

"For Zeus' name, man! Stop that thing!" cried Eurystheus and Hercules clenched his fist muting the deafening sound.

"Impressive isn't it?" he said admiring the gift that Athena had given him.

"What?" shouted king Eurystheus who couldn't hear a thing after all that noise.

"What?" said Hercules who also couldn't hear anything.

"Your labour is complete" informed Eurystheus.

"What?" yelled Hercules who still couldn't hear clearly.

"Your labour" screamed the king

"Your labour is done."

"Yes, I'm able. Well done" misinterpreted Hercules raising his thumb. "Is my labour valid now?"

"Yes! Yes!" nodded Eurystheus feeling a bit tired by this kind of conversation.

"Yes!" shouted Hercules.

"What's next?" "I'll tell you later" he gesticulated.

"What? You want an alligator?" Hercules was confused.

"No! I'll later you later" screamed Eurystheus at the top of his lungs.

"Okay. You tell me later about that alligator" nodded Hercules and left the palace to go grab a bite.

7th Chapter: The Cretan Bull

"Can you hear me now?" said king Eurystheus.

"Loud and clear" answered Hercules.

"What is my next labour?"

"Here's what I want you to do. There is wild and ferocious animal south from here, on the island of Crete. It's a great white bull with big horns. The Cretan Bull"

"Are you sure?" Hercules raised a curious eyebrow as he looked at Eurystheus.

"Of course I'm sure" answered the king.

"You really must like that jar of yours" he whispered.

"What did you say?" exclaimed Eurystheus.

"Nothing. I'm going to fetch you your bull" replied Hercules and he went down to the port to find a ship. With that, he traveled to the famed island of Crete where he was welcomed by king Minos.

"Welcome, Hercules. Words of your deeds have traveled far and wide"

"Thank you for your hospitality, king Minos." said the son of Zeus.

"How can I assist you?" asked the king.

"I'm here by king Eurystheus of Tiryns to capture your fearsome bull," told Hercules.

"Really? What a blessing! Please do take him away. That beast is destroying everything in its path. Crops, orchards, everything. No one can stop it from its frenzy" said king Minos, who allowed the hero to do whatever he wanted in order to seize the beast.

"And that is I shall do" assured him the demigod hero.

Following the trail of destruction that had been left behind by the pestering bull Hercules walked on fields and hills until he finally reached his goal. He saw the Cretan Bull blowing hot air from its muzzle and stepping frantically inside a rose garden uprooting the plants with his horns because one of the rose's thorns had pricked his leg.

"Hey! Stop that!" shouted Hercules but to no avail. The bull was on a rampage tearing flowers up and tossing dirt all around with his black hooves.

"I said stop that," said Hercules coming close and patting him in the back. The animal however was enraged and tried to stab the hero with his horns. Hercules was quicker though and immediately grabbed its horns and flipped himself into its back.

The bull wasn't easy to succumb, but Hercules wasn't an ordinary man. Using his immense strength he locked the beast's neck in his muscular arms and finally brought it down. He then tied it in a yoke and dragged it all the way to the beach.

"You have my deepest gratitude," said to him, king Minos.

"Next time I visit your beautiful island I'll stay a little longer to enjoy your delicious food" replied Hercules and boarded the ship pushing the bull inside.

When he reached Tiryns, he went with the bull straight up to the king Eurystheus' palace.

"I didn't expect anything less" sighed Hercules as he watched the king of Tiryns hurling himself again inside his storage jar.

"Help! Help me!" he cried.

"There's nothing dangerous here, my king," said Hercules.

"Take away that beast! Ah! Take it away!" he begged him.

"Its teeth aren't sharp. It's just a spoiled little bull" remarked Hercules.

"I said take it away. That horns are pointy enough to pierce me or blind me. Help!"

"Alright, alright. I'll take it away from your palace" said the hero who did what the king had asked, releasing the bull in the green fields outside Tiryns.

"I'm pretty sure it is not going to do anything violent from now on. I see it has found some of Augeas' cows to play with" noticed Hercules and went back to the palace to wait for the king to leave his jar so that he could hear his next assignment.

8th Chapter: The man-eating mares of Diomedes

For the next labour, king Eurystheus appointed a crew to Hercules in order to help him out. Our hero was to travel to the island where the man-eating mares of Diomedes were.

"Yes" said Hercules
"I am to capture more animals. You know, my king, you should change your business because the zoo you're planning on opening isn't really working. I bring animals to you and you keep letting them go"

"Don't worry, son of Zeus. One day I'll be brave enough for the animals you're fetching me" replied the king.

"Sure, and I one day will grow a third arm" laughed Hercules and left for the port. There, thirty men greeted him and welcomed him to their ship.

"By order of the king Eurystheus we will sail with you, son of Zeus" the captain informed him and Hercules warmly shook his hand accepting the help with a smile.

"Off we go!" the captain gave the order and all the men manned their posts.

After a week or so, the ship has reached the island of Diomedes. The anchor was dropped and Hercules with twenty of the men went ashore to search for the stables. It didn't take long to find them.

"Look" one of the men pointed out "There are the horses. They're tall and muscular like none I have seen before. They sure look heavy. Oh, look the bright white hair on their long bodies, their long grey mane and their sparkling blue eyes. How beautiful they are!" he noticed.

"And deadly. Don't forget, my friend that these mares feed on human flesh" added Hercules looking past them to the guards that stood vigilant. "We should draw them away"

"We need a distraction," said someone and Hercules sent three of his companions close to the stables with specific directions.

"Nay, Nay" they started to shout imitating the sound of horses.

"What's that?" the guards were confused. "Horses! Invaders!" they cried and all of them rushed towards the sound.

Hercules saw that and together with the rest of his men ran inside the stables and stole the mares. But, the guards took notice of them and quickly turned around and attacked them, with no success however, for they were facing the son of Zeus.

"Run away! To the palace!" they shouted and retreated inland.

"Quickly now, to the beach!" ordered Hercules and his companions followed him. When they saw the ship they prepared the horses to get them aboard but a strange noise halted them. It was the sound of Diomedes" advancing army that was closing on them.

"You" Hercules said looking at one of his comrades. "Hold the horses while we go and fight off the soldiers of the island" and handed him the reins of the two mares.

"And be careful" he added before he left with the sword in hand.

The battle between the army of Diomedes and the outnumbered men of Hercules was fierce and seemed to draw on all day. In the end, just before sundown, the son of Zeus was victorious, and not only that, but he had also captured king Diomedes.

"Back to the ship!" he shouted to his men. When they arrived to the beach though, they saw the two horses running wild about, restless and frantic as if struck by some madness. They were able to seize them again and Hercules wondered if his friend had got scared and ran off.

"Ha!" smirked Diomedes at his feet. "Look at the torn clothes under their hooves.That means they have eaten your friend and got very excited about it"

Hercules was enraged when he heard of this, but nevertheless he sought a way to calm the beasts.

"How am I to pacify them? I can't carry them aboard in that state"

"They will relax only if they eat human flesh again" Diomedes said and Hercules gazed at him for a minute.

"You're right" he murmured and grabbed the king by his shoulders "And there's no perfect meal than their own master" said and tossed him to the mares who ate him right away.

"Disgusting!" said the crew, but Hercules told them that Diomedes got what he deserved because for many years the king had been ruthlessly abducting poor villagers to feed his horses.

Anyway, when that was done, Hercules tied the horses' mouths just to be sure and without any difficulty carried them to his ship.

No problem occurred during the travel back to Tiryns, and when Hercules presented the mares to the king, Eurystheus, surprisingly enough, didn't cower in front of them as he usually did, although the thought of jumping in his jar did cross his mind.

"Their mouths are shut," he said bravely, and Hercules tried to tease him a bit as he went to unbind them.

"Here, my king, you can check their teeth if you like" he proposed.

"That won't be necessary!" he raised his hands.

"I believe they are perfectly fine."

"That means that we're good here?" the demigod asked.

"Yes, yes. You have completed yet another labour. Take the horses to my stables." replied the king and Hercules felt satisfied.

9th Chapter: The belt of Hippolyta

Thinking what to order him next king Eurystheus was approached by his daughter, Admete.

"Father" she glanced at him with sad eyes.
"What is it, pumpkin?" he said sensing her uneasiness.
"My birthday is coming soon, and I want a gift"
"A gift? Oh my!" frowned the king and sat down to think what he could give her daughter on her birthday.

"It must be something special. But what exactly?" he pondered and at long last, he had found the perfect present.

"Hercules" he approached the hero.

"I want you to bring me the belt of the queen of the amazons so that I can give it as a gift to my daughter"

"Amazons?" Hercules's face was grim.

"Yes, strong warrior women who…"

"I know what an amazon is" interrupted him the son of Zeus

"But I'm here, at your service, only to complete labours and not to go around shopping clothes for your daughter"

"That will be your next task unless you're afraid of some women with bows and sticks" grinned cunningly Eurystheus.

"Not more than you're afraid of a harmless boar" answered Hercules wiping off that silly grin of the king's face.

He once again went by the dock and with the same crew, he had caught the mares of Diomedes he set for the mythical land of the Amazons.

Soon enough he was on their shores and seeking an audience from the queen Hippolyta he and his men were brought to the palace. Before the demigod could say anything, the queen had already agreed to hand him the belt.

"I'm impressed with your feats over the last few years and your adventures are sure an inspiration to us all," she told him.

"Thank you, my queen," Hercules said.

"You and your men are welcomed to dine with us. At first light, I shall give you my belt and blessings for a safe journey back home"

"Thank you. Your generosity is worthy of your good fame and name, my queen" replied the son of Zeus, who took the chance to relax for once in his labours.

Hera, however, disapproving of this, had a plan of her own. Disguised as an amazon she started to spread lies among the other women.

"Hercules is an evil man" she was whispering
"He can't have come here only to take a belt. He means to kill our queen and burn our land to the ground"

Now for someone who personally knew Hercules those things mentioned were incorrect, but the amazons who didn't know him believed the lies of Hera and before the night was over they had attacked the men shouting and chanting war songs. Hippolyta couldn't avoid the conflict and soon Hera had her on her side. Swords clashed and arrows were fired. Men and women fought like dogs over sausage and Hercules and his crew barely escaped from the palace and rushed to the beach to make there their final stand.

The battle that commenced on the sands was horrible and unlike any man had ever seen. Hercules thought he couldn't survive, but like it has been said some many times before, the son of Zeus couldn't die so easily and in the end, he and his men defeated all of the amazons, and took the queen Hippolyta's belt: A beautifully crafted golden girdle with rubies, emeralds, and sapphires.

"Here's your belt," said Hercules with a heavy face as he delivered the prize to King Eurystheus. He, in turn, gave it to his daughter who was overjoyed with such a gift. But, something wasn't right.

"Daddy" she came crying to him.

"What is it, pumpkin?"

"The belt is too small for me. I can't wear it" she complained and truth be told she was right. The belt was way too small for her waist.

"Tell her to lose some weight" groaned Hercules to the king who couldn't stand hearing Admete's nagging.

10th Chapter: The cattle of Geryon

"For your next task, you will go to the island of Erytheia and fetch me the famous cattle of the three-bodied Geryon. Be wary though for the giant has a wild two-headed shepherd dog named Orthus" said king Eurystheus.

"Do the cattle have two heads or three bodies?" Hercules wanted to know.

"No, they're simple animals like any other cow or bull" answered the king.

"And why are they famous?"

"They are red"

"Red?" Hercules was puzzled. "What do you mean red?" "They have red hides, their hair is red. Red" told Eurystheus.

"Is that all?"

"Yes"

"And you want me to travel to a strange land, face a giant and his dog and fetch you some ordinary cattle?" the hero frowned.

"Exactly"

"Very well." replied the hero who as it seemed didn't have a choice.

Soon, he was dispatched to the island of Erytheia to find and capture the famous cattle of Geryon. This time, the son of Zeus traveled alone crossing the Libyan Desert to the south. The heat there was unbearable as it's always in any desert, and the sun was beating down the earth like a hot iron hammer.

"So hot!" Hercules complained and fired an arrow straight at the Sun trying to make him lower his fire. The god of the sun, Helios was impressed by Hercules' courage and for that gave him his golden cup, with which the god used to sail from west to easy in order to bring the day in the world.

Hercules reached Erytheia inside the cup and set right away to locate the cattle. The first thing he saw was Orthus, the two-headed shepherd dog of Geryon, but that he quickly eliminated with a hit from his club.

"Sleep now, rabid dog," he said and walked further inland. He didn't move far however when the giant Geryon spotted him and readied himself to attack the intruder.

"It has been a lot of time since I last fought someone. Stand where you are, stranger. Wait for me to come and kill you" he yelled and picked up his arms. He tried to wear his helmets, but since he had three bodies it took him a while to prepare properly. He was confused as to which body to arm first. He even attempted to put three breastplates on the same torso.

"Take your time, friend" smiled Hercules watching this hilarious scene, but soon he got bored and took out his bow. He forcefully drew back one of his poison arrows.

"Wait! Wait!" the giant Geryon shout

But the poison arrow fired it straight to the giant side, piercing all three of his bodies and in that way killing him swiftly. He then herded the cattle and brought it to the cup squeezing along himself in it and beginning the travel back to Tiryns.

"Thank Zeus, you're not king Augeas' animals or I wouldn't be able to feel my noise till the end of the journey," he said.

11th Chapter: The golden apples of Hesperides

"You have two more labours to complete" mentioned king Eurystheus.

"You mean one more" Hercules replied.

"No, two more" repeated the king.

"And why's that?"

"Let me remind you that the Hydra labour was invalid because your nephew

Iolaus helped you"

"That's one" said Hercules.

"Yes, but also the Augeas' stables is also not completed" added Eurystheus.

"What? But I cleaned that mess" objected the hero.

"Yes, you did, but you took money from king Augeas, which makes it kind of a service to him rather than to me. So, you have two more labours to perform"

"Fine!" Hercules shouted and waited to hear his next assignment.

"I want three golden apples from the Hesperides garden" demanded king Eurystheus.

"Where's that?" Hercules asked.

"How should I know. You're the hero here, not me." said the king and sent him off to his quest.

Hercules was unaware as to the location of that legendary garden. Athena, didn't come this time to aid, and it was Zeus himself who dressed like an old beggar came to him and revealed the way to the garden.

"Thank you, old man" said his son, not knowing he was talking to his father, who quickly told him the truth. "What?" Hercules was surprised.

"I've made a bet with Poseidon if I could fool you in those clothes and it seems I have won. The god of sea owns me now one cup of frozen nectar. Hahaha!" admitted Zeus and vanished into thin air.

"All day long, all eternity long, these gods seem to play like little children do" murmured Hercules and travelled to the garden of Hesperides. Soon enough he saw the garden and tried to reach some of the golden apples that stood dangling from the branches. But, the trees were high and Hercules couldn't reach them. He jumped and jumped and still he couldn't reach them. He was near desperation when he heard a booming laughter from afar.

He followed the echoing sound and presently came to the titan Atlas who was holding the sky on his shoulders.

"What's so funny, Titan?" asked him Hercules.

"You are, so short and weak, trying to catch those delicious apples" laughed Atlas and his laugher burst like a thunder all around him.

"Is that so?" the hero gave him an angry look.

"I can help you if you want"

"Really? How?" Hercules was curious to know.

"If you hold the sky in my stead I shall go and fetch you as many apples as you want" suggested Atlas and the son of Zeus, not seeing any other alternative, agreed.

"Hold it steady" he said as he put it on the demigod shoulders.

"I'll be back in a moment. I think" and ran off.

That last part though Hercules didn't hear. His heart was nearly pounding in his ears from the unbelievable weight of the sky pressed upon his body.

64

"My Zeus! How heavy it is! I wish Atlas comes back soon or I'll be squashed like an ant" he moaned.

In the meantime, the titan had already got the apples and was about to return to his post when a thought crossed his mind. [I'm relaxed now. Why should I turn back?] and with that thought he decided not to keep his promise to the son of Zeus.

"After all, gods and titans are born enemies. He is a demigod. His father condemned me to hold the skies. So, no. No, I'm free. Free to go wherever I please" he turned to leave.

But, Hercules saw him and realizing that he would never leave that difficult spot quickly came up with an idea.

"Hey, Atlas!" he shouted
"Ahoy, Atlas!"

"What?" the titan stopped.

"You forgot to show me how to properly hold the sky. I don't want to cause any accident and drop it. I'm not the one to be blamed for that if anything bad happens"

Atlas, still fearing the wrath of Zeus on that matter, chose to turn back to the peak where he had left Hercules and show him the right way of holding the sky.

"Alright" he said "Let me show you" and came closer. But as he came close enough, Hercules lifted the sky a bit higher and made it rest on Atlas' shoulders again.

"Ah, yes, that's the proper way to hold it. Now come back to... Hey! Where are you going?" the titan yelled, but Hercules had taken the apples and was running away from him.

"I tricked you the same way you tricked me, Atlas!" he shouted back to him thus completing the eleventh labour.

12th Chapter: The Cerberus

"Now, it's one more" said king Eurystheus when he saw Hercules approaching with the golden apples in his hands.

"Yes" answered Hercules with a heavy and tiresome voice. "What must I do now?"

"Oh, I'm sure you'll succeed in that one too" smirked ironically the king knowing and hoping at the same time deep in his heart that the son of Zeus wouldn't be able to come through that last task.

"So" Hercules interrupted him from his musings. "What's the final labour?"

"Ah, yes. I want you to bring me Cerberus, the three headed hound with the snake tail that watches over the gates of the Underworld!"

"That's easy" laughed Hercules trying to amuse his fatigue. Many years have passed since the hero undertook these formidable tasks and now that he was so close to the end he felt so tired.

He went to one of the temples dedicated to Athena and asked for guidance and assistance. The goddess of wisdom heard his plea and came to him and along her side was Hermes, the god of trade among many things and also the messenger of the Olympian gods.

The three of them entered the underworld and crossed the river Styx, the boundary between the world of the living and the world of the dead after they had paid the ferryman Charon with three gold coins. When on the other side, Hercules was given an extra coin and the two deities left him alone to complete his quest.

In the underworld the son of Zeus saw the spirits of all those who had died and some he recognized although they seem to ignore his presence. He saw the famed hero Theseus among other great men and the fearsome monster Medusa who had snakes for hair, and with a single glance could turn humans into stone. That indeed was a interesting sight, but Hercules didn't have time to sit there and idly watch the spirits of the departed. He had a purpose to fulfill.

He reached the palace of Hades, the ruler of the underworld, and asked from him to let him to capture Cerberus. Hades agreed at first, but only if the demigod hero could bring the beast down using only his bare hands. Hercules fought with the guardian hound and soon enough had overpowered it.

He then carried him on his shoulders all the way to the surface and the world of the living. It didn't took him long to reach Tiryns, and when king Eurystheus gazed at the three headed beast got so frightened that what a surprise hid inside his large storage jar again. Not sure if that was the last time he did that.

"Please, Hercules, take that monster away from me!" he begged from inside his jar.

"I will do that" said Hercules

"If you acknowledged that I have completed all of the labours that you have set for me, and I'm now redeemed"

"Yes, yes, alright" cried the king "You have atoned for your crime and can now go in peace"

Hercules was more than happy to hear that. Later on, with Hermes help, he returned Cerberus to the underworld petting him like a sweet puppy more than once on their way back as he had come to like the beast, which in return licked him to show its mutual affection.

Epilogue

Having succeeded and atoned for his crime, Hercules was invited to mount Olympus to celebrate together with the high gods his victory over the malice and jealousy of Hera. As it was, the queen of the gods wasn't there at that time, refusing to acknowledge the son of Zeus as an equal to her preferring instead to go on a vacation.

"Welcome, Hercules" shouted Zeus hugging his boy.

"Hello, father" smiled Hercules feeling as though a mountain had embraced him. The king of the gods was a large man.

"Come, come, let me introduce you to the rest of the family" he said almost dragging him to the rest of the Olympians, who sited inside a circular pillared room.

"Here's Athena and Hermes. I believe you have already met them."

"Welcome, Hercules" they greeted him.

"Artemis, you have met her as well" Zeus showed the goddess of hunt.

"Yes, how could I forget? The Ceryneian Hind of course. Is the animal okay?" asked Hercules.

"It's fine, thank you" answered Artemis politely.

"Next to him is her twin brother, Apollo, the god of music" Zeus carried on "That grumpy fellow over there who drinks alone is your brother Ares, the god of war. A good boy but always picks fights with pretty much everyone around here. I believe he is a little misunderstood"

"Who is that?" Hercules noticed a god who was beating a heavy hammer on a bronze anvil.

"Oh that, that is Hephaestus, our smithy. The god of blacksmiths, metalworkers, carpenters and everything else that involves heavy manual labour"

"Hello, Herc!" he waved at him.

"Over here is my brother Poseidon and my sister Demeter. The god of the sea and the goddess of the harvest and fertility"

"Hello, uncle" Hercules gave his hand.

"Kiss my trident, silly boy!" ignored him Poseidon and walked away.

"Don't mind him. He spends a lot of time in the sea and he's a little weird." whispered Zeus.

"How are you, my boy?" goddess Demeter said to him.

"Oh, hello, aunt. Nice to meet you" Hercules smiled at her.

"And these last two are Dionysus and Aphrodite. The god of wine and the goddess of beauty."

"Hey, Hercules!" they both cried and asked him to join him.

"In a while" said Zeus and turned to his boy.

"So, Hercules. How were your labours?"

"Long and tiresome, but interesting nevertheless" the demigod answered.

"You know, Hera did a great injustice by forcing you to commit that terrible murder, but I never stopped believing in you. I knew that you were going to succeed in your quest" Zeus rested his hand on his shoulder.

"I take it the twelve labours were inspired by you, I mean the twelve gods of Olympus?" asked Hercules.

"Oh, I don't know. Maybe." Zeus furrowed his brow.

"Anyway, I think the tasks were unique although for a few I wasn't sure I was going to make it."

"The Nemean Lion, the Hydra and the Stymphalian birds. Those you had to kill"

"Yes, I felt sorry for the lion. But it did cause a lot or trouble. Hydra was a difficult one and the birds likewise. I take it the last two were created by Hera and Ares respectively?" Hercules noted.

"Yes, you're right." Zeus ascertained.

"Then, the Ceryneian Hind, the Erymanthian Boar, the mares of Diomedes, the Cretan Bull, the cattle of Geryon, the Cerberus. All these animals I had to go and get and then release. I felt like I was babysitting a few of them. I liked that."

"And the belt of the amazon queen Hippolyta, and the golden apples of Esperides. I loved how you dealt with that arrogant Atlas"

"Yes, those two labours were hard to accomplish" said Hercules

"But, the most difficult one was to clean those disgusting stables of king Augeas"

"Dear me" exclaimed Zeus bringing up the horrible stench in his mind.

"You're absolutely right. That was a formidable task" and laughed.

"What are you going to do now?" he asked him afterwards.

"I will continue to travel around and help people" Hercules said feeling that this was the purpose of his life.

"You won't stay here with us and become a god?" Zeus pouted a little.

"I'd love to, but I see eleven gods here. Hera is away and that means a lot. I can't say I hold any grudges, but I feel that if I remain here then things will certainly go awry at mount Olympus. I don't want to unsettle you, and besides I'm more needed on earth

where there a lot of things that require my assistance"
Hercules supported his decision.

"If that's your wish, my son I can't do anything but
accept it. All I want is for you to be happy, and
always remember that if ever you need my help I'll be
there for you"
"Me too" said Athena and Hermes who had overhead
them.
"And I can forge you a new sword if you like"
Hephaestus squeezed in.
"And I can provide you with the finest wine if you
ever want to have a party" Dionysus came close.
"'Yes, we all shall lend you a helping hand" Zeus said
and before he sent his son down to earth, he hugged
him one last time.

In the course of the next years, Hercules had many
adventures fighting off evil forces and protecting
helpless men and women. His legend grew to such
heights that his name became a synonym to the word
hero, bravery, courage, endurance and strength. He

was the greatest hero of all times. The mighty son of Zeys, the demigod fighter of good, Hercules.

THE END

CHARLIE
BOOK

Printed in Great Britain
by Amazon

19895268R00051